The TOTAL(ED) PARENT

Hope for Parents Caught in the Struggle

Dave & Jan Stoop

Harvest House Publishers
Irvine, California 92714

THE TOTAL (ED) PARENT

Copyright © 1978 Harvest House Publishers
Irvine, California 92714
Library of Congress Catalog Card Number: 78-62916
ISBN 0-89081-159-8

Momma and Poppa sat on a wall.
Momma and Poppa had a great fall.
    All the king's horses
    And all the king's men
Couldn't put them *totally* together again.

Dedicated to our three sons:

Mike
Greg
Eric

Introduction

We're two of those parents who have read most everything written on how to be the complete, totally adequate, understanding and consistently successful parent. And for awhile we really believed we were just that—successful.

We should have been successful. After all, we had spent many years working with young people, counseling them, having them in our home, seeing them through their crises, talking with their parents—trying to understand. We were supposed to be the experts. And based on all that experience plus my years spent studying for a doctorate in psychology, and Jan's years spent teaching children, we felt we were pretty well equipped to raise three healthy, normal, well-behaved boys. Wow, did we ever have a lot to learn!

Fortunately, we got out of youth work before our boys became teenagers. For that's when our ideas about successful parenting met head-on with reality. And when reality hit, we fell from our cloud of confidence with a thud, We discovered we were facing problems just like those other parents had—even the ones we had privately criticized.

But then we also discovered that as we

talked with other parents about what we were facing, we didn't feel quite so alone. And we didn't feel quite so guilty. And we didn't feel so much like failures.

We've written this book, hoping that as we share some of our experiences and the experiences of some of our friends, you won't feel so alone, or so guilty, or like such a failure. After all, it can happen to anyone!

We hope that it offers help to the parents who feel they've "had it." Our intent is not to tell parents how to do it "right," but to provide a means of survival for those parents who feel they've done it "all wrong."

We've also written this book, hoping that the royalties will help us recoup some of the expenses of lost skateboards, wrecked motorcycles, lost bicycles, wrecked nerves, blown engines, lost cars, broken hearts, psychologist's bills, attorney's fees, valium prescriptions and lost sleep. The situations are factual, we've only changed the names to protect some of the guilty.

We've also discovered it is difficult for two people to write one book. The typewriter only accommodates two hands, not four. So since Dave does the typing, we tell the story from his perspective. But the ideas and the experiences have been a shared project and hopefully reflect a point of view from both a total(ed) mother and a total(ed) father.

Contents

1

Have You Hugged Your Parents Today?

Some days, anything can make a parent feel guilty—even a bumper sticker. There's one in particular that pushes my guilt button. It reads, "Have you hugged your kid today?" I remember the first time I saw that one. I calmly did a mental check back through the day and said to myself, "Yeh, I think I caught two out of three today."

Lately though, every time I see one of those on a car, I want to scream my protest: "No! I haven't! I can't hug my kid because he won't let me!!!" But the feelings don't go away. After all, parents should hug their kids. I guess I'm tired of always being made to think it's my fault.

Come to think of it, those bumper stickers are never on the cars driven by kids—only parents. Why do other kids' parents want to make me feel guilty? I'm ready to start a campaign with bold black marking pens. It's time to cross out the word, "kid" and write in "parents." I can see it now. Our son is driving down the freeway and sees one of the modified bumper stickers that now reads, "Have you hugged your parents today?" And he's filled with guilt, not me! I'm feeling better already.

❦   ❦   ❦

One peaceful morning, while calmly reading the *Los Angeles Times*, we were suddenly jarred from that day's relatively guilt-free existence. In bold black headlines, we read, "Son Says Parents Failed Him—So He Sues Them for $350,000.

"Oh, no! Quick, get our insurance agent on the phone," one of us yelled. "See if we're covered." With fear and trembling, we waited while our agent checked through our homeowner's policy. "No," he sighed, "I can't find any clause that covers malpractice of parenting."

As we read the details in the article, we looked at each other. This kid was suing *his own* parents for things any normal parent could be caught doing. We sure had done some things that upset our kids—more guilt!

"Do we have time to get our act together before they meet an attorney?" we both wondered. Questions bounced through our heads. "Will our own kids sue us?" "Which kid would it be?" "What would be the grounds—which incident?" "What if the judge never had any kids—or worse yet, what if he is a kid?" "Will parents be the next minority group?" "What's this world coming to?"

❧   ❧   ❧

Even the recent reader's survey conducted by *McCall's* magazine, which quoted the young college graduate, found that most readers were willing to blame the parents when things go wrong with kids. The pressure on parents, and the resulting guilt, only seems to increase. And when you've had the responsibility of working with other people's teenagers and have advised other parents for many years, the guilt seems to increase astronomically when things go wrong with your own kids.

❧   ❧   ❧

It was Sunday morning and we still hadn't heard from Jeff. The details were sketchy. Tuesday night he hadn't come home. By two o'clock that morning both of us were suddenly awake and knew that something was wrong. It's not as if we hadn't gone through this feeling a thousand times before. But this time we both had a feeling that this was not just another late night out for our seventeen-year-old son. We had been through four years of stress and strain, toil and trouble with him, but recently we were in a peaceful lull that had lasted for several months. We were enjoying again how much fun he was—in the fleeting moments we saw him—and he was making sounds that maybe we were still human. He had been coming in at night—sometimes an hour or two late—but coming in! This time something was different, and we both seemed to know it.

When we checked with his friends on Wednesday, we found that only one person had seen him that morning for a few minutes. He gave us a sketchy story of what Jeff had said happened. He only knew that Jeff had been in an accident; that the car had turned over and was probably totaled; that Jeff had ended up face down on the floor of the back seat; that the car had to be towed; and that JEFF WAS SCARED!

Our imagination ran wild. At least someone had seen he could still walk, but did he have any injuries? Did he need to be checked out by a doctor? Maybe he had a head injury? Could he be somewhere dazed? Why wouldn't he come home? How could he be that scared? Had we ever given him reason to be afraid to tell us *anything*?

We checked with the AAA towing services and none of them had any record of picking up the car. We called the Sheriff, several local police departments and the

Highway Patrol—no one had a record of any accident. And still no word from Jeff.

Wednesday became Thursday, and Jeff hadn't been seen again by anyone. We checked all our sources again with the same results—no car and no son. Earlier we had said, "Thank you, Lord. At least someone has seen him alive." But now our worst fears were being mixed with anger at God, Jeff and society in general. Why couldn't anyone tell us what had happened?

Finally, on Friday afternoon, the one friend who had seen Jeff remembered the name of the towing service he thought Jeff had mentioned. We had been to their office to check several times already and had drawn a blank. For some reason, I decided to drive out to their storage yard. There it sat in all its wrecked glory. At least now we knew where the car was.

Embarrassed, the owner of the towing service called his driver, who had been on duty that night. He remembered picking up the car, but had forgotten to write it in the log! "What happened to our son?" we asked. I heard his voice on the radio as he answered, "I dropped him off at the bottom of your hill."

At least Jeff had remembered where he lived, but he never made it home. We tried to imagine what had gone through his mind at the bottom of the hill. We could understand some of his apprehensions. He had just talked his older brother, Mark, into selling him his well-preserved 1967 Camaro SS—complete with mag wheels, wide tires, air shocks and powerful stereo. Mark had agreed reluctantly to accept weekly payments from him, but Jeff hadn't as of yet had time to make the first payment.

By now, both of us were living on the frazzled edge. We were really angry now! Angry at Jeff for not coming home. And angry at God for the lousy timing. Jeff had just signed up for a Young Life camping trip that seemed to mean a lot to him. We were excited because we thought it might provide some different friends that could maybe help him break out of a pattern that only seemed to be spiraling downward. We had a hard time even believing he wanted to go. This had been the first step in four years that he had taken on his own in what seemed to be a positive direction.

The trip was coming soon, and we angrily reminded God that we had asked Him to put a fence around Jeff and protect him from anything that would prevent him from going on that trip.

The mystery continued into Saturday. Suddenly, the Sunday morning Homebuilders class popped into the midst of our strung-out minds. Reality struck—"I've got to teach tomorrow morning and that's the last thing I want to think about right now," I exclaimed.

Have you ever been faced with preparing a study that's supposed to be helpful and uplifting to two hundred adults when you feel like the whole world has beat you black and blue emotionally, physically and spiritually! "Impossible," I moaned. "Why even try it?" It was too late to find someone else. "Maybe the pressure of the deadline will help in the morning," I said as I turned the light out.

Sunday morning came too quickly and no news was not good news. In two hours I would be facing all those people and I had to have something to say. "Maybe we could just sing all morning, or I could put them into small groups to share," I said to Jan, knowing that really was not the answer.

Somehow, I gathered some ideas together and we headed for church—still angry and still hurting inside. I watched the clock, hoping the preliminaries would take some extra time. They did, but I still had twenty-five minutes to take care of, and now I was in front of the class. My pride said, "Fake it. Jump right in and do the study and get it over with." I had done that before. But this time I rejected that thought and decided to share a little of what we had been through that week. At least I would have a good excuse if I blew the study.

But I wasn't ready for what happened when I finished. I don't remember how many people came up to Jan or me and said, "Hang in there. We had a son (or daughter) that went through the same kind of things. Don't give up!" These people had already been a healing influence in other areas of our lives. Now they were reaching out to us in this area of hurt. As we rode home that morning, the anger and pain seemed to subside a bit. At least if we were failures as parents, we weren't alone.

Several people sent us notes in the mail the following week, sharing in more detail some of the struggles they had been through with some of their children. We were surprised at some of the names—we had no idea they had ever had trouble with one of their kids. We thought maybe we should start a Parents Anonymous program, just so we could know we're not alone.

The end of that episode found a scared and lonely boy finally calling after two weeks, to test the atmosphere about coming home. We told him what his easygoing brother Mark had been saying all along, "Why would you think we care more about the car than we do about you?"

He came home, worked out some of the difficulties created by the police report that appeared six days later—it seems there are always some dangling ends that never get resolved in our family—and picked up where he left off. He went on the trip, and after taking two steps backwards, seems to have taken three steps forward at this point.

"Forgive me Lord, I get so impatient . . ."

It's hard to describe all the feelings you have and the questions you ask when one of your kids is missing for two weeks. Many of them relate to the struggle over how we could have done things differently. And always we struggle with the feelings of guilt.

I wonder if that young college graduate, quoted by *McCall's* magazine will feel the same way when her kids are grown. Will she still find it easy to blame parents, or will reality poke holes in her easy answers?

I also wonder who is going to help the parent who is so laden down with guilt over a troubled son or wayward daughter, that he can hardly function as a responsible adult? After all, all the king's horses and all the king's men couldn't put Humpty together again. What makes us think the fragile

resources we sometimes reach for and depend on can help put our families together
again?

Let's check our resources.

2

. . . All
the King's Men

"Most child-care advice assumes that if the parents administer the proper prescriptions, the child will develop as planned. It places exaggerated faith not only in the perfectability of the children and their parents, but in the infallibility of the particular child-rearing technique as well."

Psychology Today
February, 1978

A quick check in any bookstore offers the assurance that help is only a page or two away. There is a book that offers help for practically every human problem imaginable! Women can learn how to be assertive; men need only read to discover the secrets of success; singles can learn either how to enjoy their singleness or how to find a mate; married persons can find a book that will give them the courage to divorce, enrich their present relationship, or just about anything in between.

When it comes to help in raising children or fitting the pieces of family together, Humpty Dumpty should have had it so good. The array of resources appears to be unlimited. You can find a book on raising confident children; another on discovering and handling their temperament properly; ways to help them overcome shyness, build self-esteem, solve the unique problems presented by birth order—the list is endless. And if you don't like what one author suggests on discipline, a quick trip to the bookstore will supply you with another opinion and different advice. Everyone is so willing to tell you how to do it the *right* way.

But not all of us develop our child-rearing techniques from a book. We've all been influenced by the way our parents raised us, but we modify those ideas, not only by what we read, but also by what we see on television. Week after week, we watch the Walton family solve any and every problem that comes their way. Their kids are resourceful and respectful, and each episode ends with the children lovingly saying goodnight to each other. And when the lights go out in the house, all is peaceful and serene.

As soon as the commercial shocks us back to reality *our kids* are at it again. That is, if they're home. And in the chaos of reality, we sit and wonder why our family can't be like the Waltons. Maybe if Dad would act more like the strong, compassionate John Walton, things would be different. Or if Mom could stay home and cook a big Sunday dinner every night of the week, maybe the kids would stay home. Maybe . . . .

Perhaps your image of an ideal family

goes back to *Father Knows Best*. Remember how Robert Young would come home from the office (we assumed he worked) with a smile and a cheerful greeting. The kids would meet him at the door with a hug and a kiss. Then it was the easy chair, slippers and the newspaper, while mother finished preparing dinner. Each program portrayed a calm, peaceful family that solved all its problems, usually because the children willingly did what Father suggested and Mother was supportive. After all, Father always knew best.

However the images have been formed in our mind, we all develop a pattern of child-rearing that soon becomes a standard by which we measure everyone elses' style of raising children. We're quick to compare and judge when we see the way other parents handle their young children. As precocious little Mary pirouettes from room to room, touching things your own child isn't permitted to handle, her mother sits there silently smiling, with that "Isn't she darling" look on her face. And as we sit quietly watching each near disaster, we think to ourselves, "Wow, are they ever going to have problems with her when she becomes a teenager!" But the perspective of time says, "Maybe they will . . . maybe they won't."

❀   ❀   ❀

I suppose every parent has experienced these kinds of thoughts. A number of years ago we were in the home of some friends who had developed the seemingly remarkable—at least to us—capacity to be completely oblivious to their children's behavior. We couldn't believe the mother's calm attitude as she made only a quick comment to her one son that he should have known better than to have shot his brother in the leg with a BB gun. We sat there rather smugly thinking that we'd never let our kid get away without a spanking for such behavior and quickly put Sid and Gloria into the "permissive parents" category.

Several years later, we heard that this same son was building quite a business selling drugs on the church parking lot while his dad was preaching the sermon. We could only shake our heads and say, "What else could you expect with such permissive parents." It's so easy to pass judgment when we look at the child having problems, but how does one explain why his older brother and younger sister have blossomed into mature, vibrant young adults.

❀   ❀   ❀

On the other hand, it's just as easy to sit there and pass judgment on the parents who are so strict that even a minor act of misbehavior brings a quick response that always seems to be way out of proportion to the offense. We can remember being appalled at a mother's response to little Johnny playing with his food at the table in a resturant. A slap on the side of the head, along with the instructions, "Shut up and eat your food" was her idea of discipline.

Again, we sat in judgment thinking to ourselves, "How long will he take that? He's really going to rebel when he gets older."

❊   ❊   ❊

Ted and Mary had the same ideas about discipline, only they stopped using capital punishment when their daughter Linda got to junior high age. Drill team put a lot of demands on Linda's time, and one Saturday morning she stopped to talk with a friend and was thirty minutes late getting home from practice. She was immediately placed on a weeks restriction, even to the point of missing the next drill team practice. When she questioned the fairness of her punishment, her father grounded her for an additional two weeks to punish her for her complaining attitude. We were thinking, "Wow, that's pretty strong punishment for what she did."

❊   ❊   ❊

In the strict-vs-permissive debate, we've always thought of ourselves as being somewhere near the center of the road. But more and more we've discovered that most parents feel that they, too, have hit the balance point between strictness and permissiveness, regardless of where we feel they should be placed on our scale.

This really hit home when Al and Peggy brought their son Terry to me for counseling. Terry was the younger of their two boys and was becoming the focal point for increasing tensions within their family. I listened carefully as Al described why he was so disappointed in Terry.

The problems seemed to revolve around Terry's unwillingness to jump at his father's command. It quickly became apparent to me that Al belonged in the overly-strict category—according to my scale. I felt it was obvious that his demands were unreasonable and that his expectations were too high. I resisted the temptation to offer to exchange his son for our son; his problems for our problems. As the counseling session continued, it became clear that Al and Mary felt that their approach to raising children was one of balance, and even a bit on the lenient side. And when they described Terry's older brother, they felt justified, for he had responded positively to their discipline and met their highest expectations.

As we talked, I became aware that Al and Peggy were just another example of two parents searching for the "right" way to raise their children. We would all like to believe there *is* some formula for raising children that would inoculate them against the possibility of misery and failure as young adults.

People of some cultures assume that either fate or the "gods" are the major influence in the development of their children. Others believe it comes with social or economic status, either inherited or attained, or is provided by living in the right neighborhood or community. But most of us today are placing our faith in a properly orchestrated set of parental actions that we hope will insure our child's developmental success.

❋ ❋ ❋

I was sitting at lunch with two men. One was a tough administrator at a local college, the other a member of the faculty. As we talked, I shared with them some of the pain I was feeling trying to relate to our son. At the time, we were in the midst of one of our crises.

As I paused, taking time to eat, Clayton, the college vice-president said, "Dave, I know what you're feeling. But hang in there! My wife and I went through seven years in the desert with our son."

I almost choked on my sandwich. "You had problems with your son?" I asked, unbelieving. Then I listened as he shared some of the struggles he and his wife experienced with their boy. For seven years the battle raged before a workable truce was reached. This man, who ran such a tight ship at the college, was just now seeing some positive changes in his son's life. I sat silently, thinking that if it could happen to Clayton, it could happen to anyone.

❋   ❋   ❋

While the experts debate, families of every sort continue to struggle with the harsh realities of parenting. And it doesn't seem to matter whether a parent is strict or permissive, strong or passive, consistent or inconsistent, loving or aloof, some children respond while others rebel.

It also doesn't matter whether the child is the oldest, the youngest, or somewhere in-between. Even the middle-child syndrome cannot take the complete blame, for each family's experience is unique. Sometimes it's the oldest; sometimes the youngest.

A parent may follow some expert's advice right down the line and have no problems with any of their children. Some other parent will use the same principles for raising children and experience nothing but grief and agony.

The one consistent principle we've found is that none of the experts have the complete answer. What works for one family with one of their kids may not work with another child and may even antagonize that other child to the point of utter frustration and rebellion. Even consistency, that treasured quality, may be counter-productive, as it masks and hides some of our genuine feelings and needs.

If the experts can't help us put the pieces together again, *what's a parent to do?*

3

My Doctor Wonders Why I Need Something for Tension

"Many people find it easy to be parents, until they have children. Not long after, they scream for help. 'I feel like bashing her head against the wall or putting her in a foster home. What kind of a mother am I to have such thoughts.' "

Human Behavior
September, 1978

When the phone rings at three o'clock in the morning, and part of your family is on the opposite side of the country, all kinds of things race through your mind as you stumble for the phone. But I wasn't in any way prepared for what I heard on the other end of the line.

"I can't hear your rock band," the mysterious voice said.

"What?" I asked.

"What's the matter? I can't hear the music!" he continued.

When I explained that I didn't have the foggiest idea what he was talking about, the caller realized it wasn't Jeff on the phone, it was me—his father. That opened Pandora's box, as far as he was concerned. All of his pent-up frustration was released on me via the telephone company.

I had returned home from vacation a week earlier than the rest of the family because I had to get back to work. Jeff had talked us into letting him stay at home while we took a trip to the East Coast to visit relatives. He needed to attend summer school and wanted very much to take driver's education. In the few hours I had already been home, I had made several discoveries that led me to believe that the older fellow we had paid to stay and watch both the house and Jeff had really done nothing more than watch.

Our fifteen-year-old son had obviously driven the family car—illegally. Who knows how many miles he drove for it had never entered my mind to make a note of the mileage before we left. Summer school, which included his precious driver's training, fell by the wayside within the first week when he quickly found that the freedom and excitement of doing what he wanted was a pleasant replacement for the dreary discipline of classes.

But the phone call had my curiosity up. The voice on the other end of the line refused to identify himself, but mentioned a party. And then he added something about the Sheriff coming to break up the party. With that bit of information, the caller decided it was time for him to go back to bed, perhaps satisfied with the knowledge that I would spend a sleepless night trying to figure out what else had happened.

Since Jeff wasn't willing to volunteer any information that next morning, I visited the sheriff's station. "Oh, yes," the deputy at the desk said. "I was there that night. There were at least 500 or maybe even 600 kids there. But they cleared out within an hour after we arrived."

I could hardly believe what I was hearing. We lived in an older section of town where the yards were especially large, but even at that, it would have been wall-to-wall kids.

"Yes," the deputy continued. "He had quite an evening. Had a live band and everything—literally! They were charging admission before we came, but we had to put a stop to that."

As I walked out, shaking my head in disbelief, I could at least understand the motives behind my middle-of-the-night caller. But my Jeff? Incredible! How could he do such a think! Gradually, my disbelief changed to feelings of anxiety about what else he did while we were gone. And I felt an increasing anger at the flippant way he had disregarded his responsibilities.

As I checked around the house, I decided to wait until Jan returned home before describing to her the dents in the car, the mysterious absence of our flowers and

bushes, the cigarette burns in the uphol-
stery, the sprouts of marijuana in the back
yard, and the disappearance of several
items from within the house.

Each day I discovered more details about
the things that had gone on while we were
away, and my anger became mixed with
frustration, hurt and a growing fear of what
I might yet find out. So many things could
have happened—there could have been a
fire, he could have hit someone with the car,
and who knows what else. It tooks us quite a
while to sort it all out, and to deal with our
feelings about what did happen.

❧　　❧　　❧

Following the party, the tensions continued to build. Twice that fall Jeff ran away
from home. The first time he left, there was
no crisis or confrontation that preceded his
leaving. I was out of town, speaking at a
retreat in Florida.

The weekend had been a rough one for
Jan. Soon after I left for the airport, she
received a strange phone call asking questions, including how long would I be gone.
Since she felt uneasy, she asked the boys to
stay close to home, and they agreed. But
that Friday night, Jeff simply didn't come

home.

All night long, Jan lay awake wondering about the noises of a lonely night—was it Jeff finally coming in, or could it be a noise related to the strange phone call? When morning finally came and she gave up on sleep, she discovered our faithful watch-dog cowering on the porch, unable to walk because of an injured leg.

Her imagination ran wild. Was Jeff injured someplace? Had someone tried to break into the house, only to be scared off by the dog? Had they kicked her in self-defense? Why wasn't Jeff home?

When I returned home on Monday, he was still gone. In fact, he didn't come home for a week. The mysteries of the phone call, strange noises, and the injured dog were never solved. But at least Jeff came home. His only explanation was that his friend had been kicked out of his house and he needed someone to keep him company. We could hardly believe his reasoning.

While he was gone, I shared with a friend what was going on at home. Her husband had been one of my professors in seminary. Tears started welling up in her eyes as she encouraged us to "hang in there." Then she told me her youngest daughter had just returned home after being away for six years. Six years!

"Did you know where she was?" I asked.

"No," she answered. "She just took off and for six years we didn't know whether she was dead or alive. We heard nothing until two months ago, when out of the blue she called us and announced she was coming home for a visit. And, as incredible as it seems, she acted as if nothing had happened."

"Six years!" I repeated to myself. I thought of the ache in my heart after only five days of an empty bedroom at our house, and wondered how anyone could survive the multiplication of that pain over six years! Six years—I sat in her husband's classes during that time and never knew how much he must have been hurting!

"How could you handle all of that?" I exclaimed. She could only shrug her shoulders and say, "Somehow you just do."

❋ ❋ ❋

It was one o'clock in the morning. Rob still wasn't home. His mother paced the floor alone, for her husband was out of town on business. It seemed that everytime he had to be away lately, something would go wrong with one of the kids.

Jane had pieced together most of what happened that evening. Rob was supposed to pick up his sister at ten o'clock, but he had fallen asleep and his younger brother had trouble waking him up. He kept after him, and finally, about the time he was to meet his sister, Rob stumbled out of bed to his car and left.

Jane came home from her meeting about ten-thirty, just in time to answer the phone. Her daughter asked where Rob was. He hadn't shown up yet and she still needed a ride home. Jane left to pick her up, expecting to find Rob there by then, or at home when she returned. But that was over two hours ago, and he still wasn't home.

Had he been in an accident? Did he take off somewhere with one of his friends? She didn't know whether to be angry or worried. Suddenly, the front door opened. It was 1:10 a.m.!

"What happened? Where have you been?" Jane yelled while she also checked to make sure both his arms and legs were in one piece.

"I can't find my car, Mom. I don't know where it is."

"You what?" Jane responded incrediuiously.

"I lost my car," Rob meekly explained.

As Jane questioned him, his answers were so inconsistent and his thoughts so disorganized, she finally said in exasperation, "Go to bed. We'll figure this out in the morning!"

Sleep eluded Jane—she was angry and confused. Rob didn't appear to be hurt, but why did he act so strange. Was he trying to cover something up? After all, one doesn't lose something as large as a car.

But the next morning, Jane discovered it *was* possible to lose a car. Rob and friend had been experimenting with some home-brewed drugs that afternoon. And even though Rob's friend had no extreme reaction to the drug, Rob slept all evening and was in a trance-like state when his brother tried to wake him. When he went to pick up his sister, he became disoriented, got out of the car to find a phone, and then really did lose his car! Somehow, two hours later he ended up at home.

It took a week of family and friends spending every spare minute looking everywhere before the car was found. It was a frustrating week, for where does one begin to look for a car when Rob couldn't even remember the slightest detail about where he had been.

But the real point of tension and stress came, not with the loss of a car, but with the realization that Rob had made an irrational and irresponsible decision to experiment with a drug that could have ended his life. We had read in the newspaper just that same week that an adult trying the same drug had died from it. And the timing was so bad—Rob had been doing so well. For the past six months he had been involved in the leadership group in the youth program at church. Regular Bible discussions with one of the youth leaders seemed to be turning him in the right direction. But now this . . . Why now?

Jerry seemed like a neat kid. His dad was struggling to maintain some kind of communication with him, but each day he felt he was losing ground and losing touch with Jerry.

Most of Jerry's problems seemed to be tied to the typical adolescent struggle for independence. But the pain it caused his mom and dad hurt deeply. His parents joined forces with us to really pray for our kids and to encourage each other.

Frequently his dad would relate details of their latest crisis and then add something like, "But I don't know how you do it, Dave. Jeff keeps giving you a worse time. I couldn't survive what you're going through."

"Yes you could," I assured him, "because you *are* going through what I'm going through. The pain you feel is just as real to you as the pain I feel is real to me." I went on to tell him about the profound lesson our doctor had taught us about the relativity of the depth of hurt.

When we had reached one of our low points, and our emotional stress was at an all-time high, Jan made an appointment with her doctor to get something to help her sleep. He began asking questions about the possible sources of tension, and when Jan started telling him some of the things going on in our family, he hung on to every word.

As she finished, he sat down and began to share with her the grief and hurt he and his wife had been through with their youngest son. He was a talented young man—an artist. His paintings were hanging on every wall in his dad's office as reminders of his potential. But as he finished high school, he seemed troubled and struggled with making the right choices. At the age of 19, he committed suicide.

Jan kept thinking to herself as he talked, "How can I possibly complain about my tension and sleeplessness when I haven't been through anything like he's been through." But the more he talked, the less Jan felt that way, for it came through loud and clear that he cared, and that he understood what she was feeling. He never wondered why she needed something for tension; he knew—he'd been there. He never allowed the possibility of comparing his hurt to ours, *for he understood the relativity of the depth of hurt; we were only beginning to understand.*

We've thought about what we learned from our doctor many times—especially when we hear what some other parents have been trhough. It appears that the feelings that surround the struggles we have as parents are all relative. Only that doctor's son could hurt him so deeply. Only your son or daughter can hurt you that way. Only our children have the ability to tear our emotions apart.

So what IS a parent to do? Wait? Hope? Pray? How long? Do we simply try to hold ourselves together until they grow out of it? After all, isn't there a promise in Proverbs— that if we do a good job with our children when they are young, they will turn out alright when they get older?

4

How Old Do They Have to Get?

"Train up a child in the way he should go: and <u>when he is old</u>, he will not depart from it."

Proverb 22:6 (KJV)

We've always hung on to that promise in Proverbs. I don't know how many times I've quoted it to a hurting, worried parent, adding my own experience as an adolescent to its interpretation. I did my share of rebelling while in high school. In fact, my mother still doesn't want to know about all the things I did. But I eventually got it out of my system and got on with living. As a result, I would often use my own experience to expand the meaning of Proverb 22:6 and add, "If he does depart while a youth, it's only for a time. When he gets older he'll get back on the right track."

If this is the promise of the proverb, how old do they have to get before they find their way back to the right track?

Several months ago we met Tim and Audrey through a mutual friend. They are a bit older than we are. In fact, their two grandchildren are about the same age as our boys.

As we talked, the conversation got around to the kids, as usual. We discovered that their two grandchildren—both teen-agers—were living with them. And they expected that they would continue to have them living with them for an indefinite time.

Their son and daughter-in-law were in the midst of a divorce. But Audrey was quick to point out that their son John had been a problem for years. Neither John nor his wife wanted the kids living with them— they were too wrapped up in solving their own problems. And John was acting just like a teenager! All he could talk about was "finding himself," and he was convinced he had to do that alone.

"Don't they ever grow up," Tim asked with a tired sigh. "He's 37 years old and it seems like all we do is help him out of a jam only to see him get tied up in some other mess somewhere else."

Divorce is never simple. It always brings pain and hurt to all parties involved. But Bill's divorce is even more painful, for he continues in an adolescent-like rebellion against his wife, God, his parents, and even his own kids. How much older does he have to get? Sure makes a parent wonder.

❀   ❀   ❀

Jim and Marian have always been special to us. When we were attending college, Jim was on the faculty there and was so well respected that he became a legend at the school. After several years of teaching there, he and Marian moved to the West Coast, where he took a position on the faculty of another college.

We were excited when we moved to California, and the discovery that Jim taught a special Wednesday night class at the church where I would be working was a special treat. While I studied for my ordination exams, he volunteered to stay late on Wednesday evenings to help me with some of my questions.

About a year later, he returned to the East Coast, and we kept in touch for awhile directly and then through mutual acquaintances. Before returning to the East, Jim and Marian had some difficult times with their youngest son. He got caught up in the counter-culture of the late 1960's and started experimenting with various drugs.

For ten years, Jim and Marian struggled, using every available means of help to nurture their son back to good mental health. But the doctors said that his mind will never be the same. For ten years they have lived in the uncertainty of what their son might do next. He is totally unpredictable!

Why? Why Jim and Marian's son? For years they have given of themselves to help train and develop the minds of young people. For years they have kept a balance between their outside involvements and their commitment to their own children. It seemed so unfair that they should lose their son to the mindlessness created by a drug.

Recently, Jim decided to accept a teaching position at a college in England. Their son was interested in going with them and even seemed excited about the possibility of a new environment. Visas were all in order and everything was packed. But the night before they were scheduled to leave, their son left home and was swallowed up in the underground of his drug-addicted friends.

Travel was delayed while Jim and Marian did everything they could to find him, but to no avail. Finally, with broken hearts and bodies bent almost beyond endurance by pain and sorrow, they left. After all, their son was now 28, and how old does he have to get? How long do John and Marian have to wait to see an answer to their prayers?

❊   ❊   ❊

Jenny's a beautiful gal. When you meet her, you're immediately drawn to the beauty of her face and the sparkle of her personality.

Her dad's a minister, but they haven't moved around alot, so you can't trace her problems to that common scapegoat. Her difficulties surfaced while in high school. She suddenly dropped her old friends and started running with a different crowd, and they had the reputation of playing around with drugs.

Her parents patiently did everything they could to affirm their love to her. They even sent her away to live with relatives, at her own request, hoping the change of environment would help. But a week later, her boyfriend sent her money for a plane trip home, and she conned a neighbor into taking her to the airport while the family she was staying with were out. They thought she was at work—she had just started a neat job the day before—but that evening they discovered that they'd all been had. That was seven years ago.

Several years of turmoil followed. Her dad drove her several hundred miles each week to keep an appointment with a special therapist. He seemed to help Jenny a bit, but the problems continued.

Brian, her old boyfriend, became the focal point of her struggles. She had a running debate with herself about seeing him and finally decided to give in and marry him.

For a while it looked like Jenny had finally broken out of the old patterns. She and Brian settled down several hundred miles away from her parents, so little was known about how they were doing. Letters home told only about the positive things, like Brian's work and the money they were saving to buy a house.

Two years later Jenny was home again— planning her divorce from Brian. And gradually, all the pain and hurt of a miserable marriage was laid out on the table. Since then she seems to have a better handle on life, but does that mean she's finally old enough to get back on the right track?

I was sitting at coffee with several friends. Gradually everyone headed back to work—coffee break time was over. Wendy seemed to want to stay. Preoccupied with her own thoughts, she still managed to ask me how Jeff was doing. I shared some of the struggles we were caught in at the moment and then noticed her eyes were filled with tears.

"What's wrong?" I asked.

"It never ends," she said bitterly, and then got up and left the table, weeping.

I didn't think I had said anything to cause the flood of tears, but I was still concerned. Later, I saw her sitting almost in the same place, with the same absentminded look in her eyes.

"Can you talk about it?" I cautiously asked.

"Oh, it wasn't anything you said," she assured me. "John and I have just been through a terrible weekend trying to knock some sense into our son's head. He came home Friday and announced he was leaving his wife." Then with tears rolling down her cheeks again, she added, "Why can't he see what he's doing? He's hurting his lovely wife—and us—and he doesn't even seem to care. Dave, I guess your kids just never stop hurting you, no matter how old they get!"

❀   ❀   ❀

When you're in the midst of the struggle with your own teenager, your faith isn't encouraged very much when you listen to parents like Wendy. No matter how many times you've heard others say, "Oh, he'll grow out of it by the time he's twenty or twenty-one," the fear remains that it could go on and on.

Little has been written explaining the meaning of the last part of Proverb 22:6— "When he is old . . .," but much has been said about the training part of the verse. Traditionally, we've been taught that if we train a child to go in the right direction, we'll get the right results.

Recently, several books have been written taking us back to the original idea, translating the verse more literally to read, "Train a child according to his way." This interpretation implies, it seems, that the training should be done with respect for a child's individuality and temperament.

But as Jan and I read through the book of Proverbs, we were amazed at some of the other things we read about parent-child relationships. It became obvious that even the best training cannot instill wisdom but can only encourage a child to make the right choices. We both smiled as we read, "It's no fun to be a rebel's father" (Proverb 17:21). How true that is! We also read, "There are those who curse their father and mother, and feel themselves faultless despite their many sins" (30:11, 12) and, "A man who robs (runs through their money) his parents and says, 'What's wrong with that?' is no better than a murderer" (28:24).

There we sat in the middle of the book of Proverbs. We felt it was written just for us. But we still didn't have an answer to the question, "How old do they have to get?"

About the time we were resigning ourselves to the possibility that our struggles could go on forever without our ever seeing things turn around, we received a letter that seemed to confirm that possibility.

Sally wrote to say that the week before, her eighty-year-old Uncle Richard had died. Her uncle's father was her grandfather, who was a great Christian man and had died some fifty years ago. When he died, his biggest concern and greatest disappointment was that his oldest son, Richard, was a rebellious young man who caused much hurt and anger, both in his family and in his circle of friends. Her grandfather's heart was broken many times by his son's selfish willfulness.

About twenty-five years ago, God tapped her Uncle Richard on the shoulder and created a new man. He became a beautiful Christian who touched many lives. At his funeral, Psalm 1 was read at the request of his many friends. They felt that his life these recent years was best described by the psalmist's words:

"Oh, the joys of those who . . .delight in doing everything God wants them to and day and night are always meditating on his laws and thinking about ways to follow him more closely."

She went on to say, "I can't help but think what a great reunion there is in heaven right now as my grandfather greets his son. In life there was so much sorrow and hurt between them, and now they meet in victory and love to share God's glory."

She finished her letter by saying she just wanted to share how God had answered her grandfather's prayers, even if it did take fifty-five years. The promise remains!

5

Ironing out the
Wrinkles of Guilt

". . . the brutal contrast between the dream and what came out of it weighs upon us as a mass of guilt."

Paul Tournier
Guilt and Grace

What parent is not disappointed in himself, at least to some degree. We all have our dreams and hopes of what a family should be—and what our children should be like. But as they grow up, they seldom fit the mold we've created within our minds. We know how they "should act," but when we are faced with the contrast between our dreams and reality, guilt wells up within.

Often, we try to reassure ourselves by recalling all the good "things" we did do. Or we blame our parents for the way they raised us, our spouse for not supporting us, our job, or any number of other forces at work in our family. But somehow the guilt persists.

If the failure to see our dreams realized does not produce guilt, then the idealized dreams of others will do the job. These people would want us to believe that the course of our nation, and even our entire civilization, could be determined by the quality of our relationships with our children. Wow! What a responsibility!

If the future of our society hinges on the way I treat my kids, we're in trouble. After all, how many parents would drag their son to the sheriff's station and say, "Here, you take him. Do something with him because I can't!" I did, and the guilt and feelings of being a failure as a parent became totally oppressive by the time we returned home an hour later.

Of course, by the next day, I had managed to bottle up all those guilt feelings. After all, most of us are willing participants in the conspiracy of silence surrounding our feelings about our roles as parents. We might joke about it, but seldom do we face the reality of our guilty conscience. And so the spiral of guilt spins on.

I can understand those feelings of guilt, for they are valid. I *was guilty*, for I overreacted. All of us are guilty, at times, of overreacting, of accusing wrongly, of punishing unfairly, or even guilty of not being sensitive and not paying attention to the entire context of a situation.

But why is it that I sometimes feel guilty for doing what a parent is supposed to do? The other night I had to say "No" to Jeff when he asked to use the family car. His truck was not running as is usually the case—and he had not been able to find a friend to pick him up. For the umpteenth time, I explained that we had to exclude him from the insurance policy on that car in order to keep the insurance. Because of his driving record, he could only be covered on one specific vehicle. He knew that and finally resigned himself to a boring evening, stuck at home.

Every time he walked into the room with a bored look on his face, guilt feelings hit me from every corner. I knew I was doing the right thing, but why did I feel so guilty? Because Jeff was unhappy! And I, like so many other parents, felt it was my job to make him happy. Happiness is always related to a series of happenings. When things run smoothly, we're happy. And I was interfering with Jeff's smooth-running series of happenings.

The love trap snaps early and catches a parent in the jaws of feeling the responsibility for making his child happy. From the time a child first asserts his own will, we struggle with the possibility of our destroying his happiness.

This has not always been true. For centuries children were severely, often brutally treated by their parents, all in the name of virtue. Play was considered frivolous and unnecessary. Work or study, depending on the family's economic status, was purposely designed to be long, hard and difficult.

During the early 17th century, parents in Europe and in the American colonies were being advised by the "experts" to beat their children in order to tame their spirit. And respected, well-educated parents often inflicted severe punishment upon their children—punishment that would be considered child abuse today.

The French philosopher, Rousseau, was probably the first major voice raised in opposition to the brutal ways children were treated. He prescribed a new formula to parents for successful child rearing, when he said that a mother's love would cure society's ills. He asserted that childhood should be a happy time and play should be encouraged. He went so far as to say that the words "obey" and "command" should be banned from use with children.

The fires of change started by Rousseau were fanned through the century that followed. Others, including John Locke and Horace Bushnell, joined the revolution. But it took the leadership of Freud to get the bonfire really blazing. Freud drew an image of the child as being extremely vulnerable. Children are sensitive beings, easily damaged by traumatic events and stress on the one side; and by overdoses of parental love on the opposite side.

Soon, parents were walking on eggs. Children literally took charge of their parents. Parents were afraid to confront their child for fear that the child would feel rejected and humiliated. Parents were to be gentle, sensitive to the innocent thoughts and feelings of the child and to protect him from any possible trauma.

Following close behind the ideas of Freud in laying a guilt trap for parents were the behaviorists. They said that the child's mind is a *tabula rasa*, or blank slate. The child is not vulnerable, they assert; he is malleable. The task of the parent is to properly shape and mold the child. The parent becomes a trainer, making certain that everything written on the blank slate of a child's mind leads to happiness and the feeling of being loved.

The behaviorists provided a structure that promised to avoid the excesses of the permissiveness proposed by the followers of Freud. The parent was still to avoid the use of punishment, but now his important task was to *train* the child by rewarding the *desired* behavior. Hence, the label: Behaviorists.

Soon, refrigerators across America were covered with charts, filled with stars and check marks indicating rewards for jobs well done. If a child didn't perform, he didn't get a star or a smiling face on his chart. Stars were tallied at the end of the week and allowances were doled out accordingly.

Whether a parent bought the ideas of Freud or of the behaviorists, he was faced with a tremendous task either way. Unless he did the right things at the right time, the child would turn out to be an unhappy and unsuccessful adult. Obviously, if something goes wrong with one of the children, according to these traditions the parents have only themselves to blame.

Our need to succeed in our role as parents blends right into the already existing tensions created by a success-oriented society. Our fear of failure is like a fog surrounding our feelings of guilt, making it practically impossible for us to see the difference between valid guilt, and that false guilt imposed upon us by society.

Any problem with our children brings to the surface those constantly present fears about failure that in turn stir up feelings of guilt that penetrate every area of our life.

Guilt paralyzes us. It threatens to rupture every relationship. It affects the relationship between husbands and wives; how we relate to the people we work with, our neighbors, and it even affects our relationship with the other children in our family.

Unless we are able to iron out the wrinkles of guilt and deal with it openly and directly, we will be caught on the hook the rest of our lives. For guilt hangs us up and removes the joy from life. The answer is not to soothe our guilty consciences, but to sort out the causes of our guilt and deal with it from that perspective.

When we have valid reasons for feeling guilty, the only solution is to ask for forgiveness. The psalmist David talks a great deal about his feelings of guilt for his failures—modern man's synonym for sin. In Psalm 51, he vividly describes the agony of his guilt and his desperate cry for forgiveness. Part of the healing process comes with the admission of his wrong action. He writes:

"O loving and kind God, have mercy, Have pity upon me and take away the awful stain of my transgressions. Oh, wash me, cleanse me from this guilt. Let me be pure again. For I admit my shameful deed—it haunts me day and night . . . give me back my joy again."

The healing process continues as we not only ask God for his forgiveness but also ask our children for their forgiveness. For without forgiveness, there would be no family. The difficulty often comes after we have done both of these things and are left only with the task of forgiving ourselves. This most difficult part of forgiveness is a necessary part of the healing process if life is to go on and the joy of living is to return.

❈ ❈ ❈

In our family, we wrestle with all kinds of feelings of guilt. Some valid, some not. When we were at a low point, and our relations with Jeff had been bumping the bottom for over a year, Jan wondered—did she cuddle him enough as a baby; did he get the right vitamins; did she pay too much attention to his brother; did we take his bottle away too soon; maybe she should have breast-fed him longer, etc. I wondered if maybe his first grade teacher was part of the cause—or did we move too many times when he was young? Did I put too much pressure on him to keep up in school or to participate in sports. Maybe I should have coached his Little League team, instead of sitting in the stands.

The list was endless. One of the things that really triggers Jan's guilt is the fact that she doesn't enjoy cooking. The thought always haunts her that maybe we didn't have enough roast beef dinners together at home. But just recently, it was enlightening to hear a girl friend of one of our boys tell Jan that all she hears from our son is what a great cook Jan is and about the really neat meals she prepares. She even went so far as to ask for some of her recipes. Jan stood there with a blank look and said, "He said WHAT?"

That was somewhat of a help in our seeing that the perspective of a child is often not the same as that of the parents. If we could only talk more about the things that make us feel guilty as parents, we might find out that maybe the child didn't suffer and wasn't deprived in his early years. If we could even talk more to our kids about these feelings, we might be surprised at what we would discover. Yet we so often remain silent and allow the guilt to fester when we see our child unhappy. We somehow still feel that the responsibility to make him happy is ours.

Someone once said that our job as a parent is to provide love, food and shelter—his basic needs. *It is not* our job to provide happiness. That's *his* job!

❀   ❀   ❀

Recent studies in child development increasingly suggest that the child has more to do with his development than we've given him credit for. We have greatly exaggerated the power of the parent and the helplessness of the child. The child's own needs influence the way he interprets every life situation he encounters. This is not to say that the parent does not have an influence on the child—he very definitely does. But we must be careful to distinguish between influence and control. One cannot control another person even if that person is a child. Every child is a unique person with a unique personality created by God, possessing a will and the freedom to choose how he interprets life. We can only be an influence.

For instance, a young child may interpret his parents' leaving him with a baby sitter as rejection. Therefore, this child may reason, "I will not attach myself to anyone because they leave me, and I must have done something wrong to cause it." As a result, he keeps himself aloof, and doesn't show his feelings. Another child, in the same situation, will reason, "I must never do anything wrong or else people will leave me and reject me." Thus he creates an unreasonable pressure on himself to always be good. Again, another child might look forward with anticipation to the return of his parents and go about having fun playing games with the baby-sitter. Of course, all three of the responses are possible in the same child on three different occasions, depending on how he feels at the moment and how he perceives events surrounding the arrival of the baby-sitter. *Perception governs behavior.*

※　　※　　※

One study at the University of California followed 200 children from infancy through adolescence and then interviewed them again at age thirty. They expected to find that children from troubled homes would be unhappy adults and that calm, happy homes would produce successful and happy adults. They were wrong in over two-thirds of their predictions. Instead, they found that many of those raised in the best circumstances turned out to be unhappy, immature and maladjusted adults. And the trauma of unhappy homes did not produce the expected result—unhappy adults. Most children who grow up in an atmosphere of disorder and early sorrow or trauma still turn out to be adequate adults. Maybe the child is not as vulnerable as we think.

Erik Erikson was once asked why so many people have overcome the effects of truly awful homes. He answered by pointing to the multiplicity of influences in a person's life—peers, teachers, other adults, etc. The question could be reversed with the same answer: Why do so many people from happy homes become unhappy adults struggling every inch of the way? Because of the multiplicity of influences in a person's life and their perception of those influences!

If we are not as powerful in our control over our children's destiny as once believed, then maybe it's time to relax a bit. Maybe our children can survive even with us as parents!

❊　　　❊　　　❊

I think one of the best examples of poor parenting is found in the Bible. Isaac was a wealthy man when he married Rebekah. He was a man blessed by God according to Genesis 25:11. And Rebekah was chosen to be his wife because of her beauty and her thoughtfulness in offering to draw water for the servant of Abraham and for his camels. (See Genesis 24.)

After twenty years of marriage, Isaac and Rebekah finally had children—twins. And "... *as the boys grew, Esau became a skillful hunter, while Jacob was a quiet sort who liked to stay at home. Isaac's favorite* was Esau, because of the venison he brought home, and Rebekah's favorite was Jacob" (Genesis 25:28, 29).

Now any parent knows you're asking for trouble when you play favorites with your children. And if you play favorites because of what a child can do for you, the troubles are compounded. But that's exactly what Isaac and Rebekah did.

The story doesn't end there. In fact, it gets worse. And soon we are in the middle of a very sordid scene, with Isaac dying on his bed and Rebekah directing the drama of lies and intrigue to make certain her favorite son receives the blessing of his father. While Esau is out hunting the venison for his father's last meal, Rebekah orders Jacob to disguise himself as Esau while she prepares a meal for Isaac out of goat meat, seasoned to taste like venison. Rebekah's plan succeeds, but Jacob is forced to flee for his life. What a mess!

I cringe inwardly as I read the account, for here are two parents using the children to get what they want. They played favorites, pitting one son against the other. As a result, the whole family must have been divided. Any objective observer could look at the family and point out all kinds of things that were wrong.

We don't know anything about whether

Rebekah felt any guilt over her behavior as a mother or whether Isaac struggled with feelings of guilt over his attitude towards Jacob. What we do know is that when God chose to identify himself to the Jewish people, he said he was the God of Abraham, *Isaac*, and *Jacob*! In spite of Isaac's failures as a parent and Jacob's problems and struggles growing up, God still valued them as persons and used their names as a point of identity.

Wow! My value as a person goes way beyond my success in my role as a parent. My identity does not depend on what I did or did not do as a parent. With that insight, I can begin to cut through the fog of guilt and see not only my own unique worth as a person but also the unique individuality of each of our children.

6

Dismiss the Behavior and Hang on to the Person

Behavior—why does he have to be so obnoxious? Why can't she use just a little common sense? He surely can't know what he's doing to himself. She just must not care what anybody thinks! Every totaled parent has these thoughts over-and-over again. And part of what upsets a parent so much is the nagging feeling that underneath that terrible behavior is a purpose and a direction. We not only fear where that purpose and direction might take him, we also feel hurt because we believe the behavior is aimed at us.

Judy was the only daughter in a family of five, and she thoroughly enjoyed all the benefits that went with her special position.

While in junior high, she developed into a delightful young woman—adored by her parents, spoiled by her brothers, appearing to have her world on a string.

Then came high school. Even her friends couldn't understand what happened. She became a moody recluse, spending all her time hibernating in her room. Sometimes she even refused to come out for dinner, sneaking food from the kitchen after everyone else had gone off to bed. When she did join the family for dinner, she sat eating in silence, glaring at anyone who might dare talk to her. The holidays came and went, and the walls Judy continued to build around herself only grew higher. Communication was almost non-existent and this was particularly painful to Caroline, Judy's mother.

Judy's behavior and appearance violated every image in Caroline's mind of what a sweet young lady should be like. But Caroline's patience astounded everyone around her. She seemed to be the perfect mother, hardly deserving a daughter like Judy. She and her husband tried everything, including talking with Judy's teachers and friends to try and understand her behavior. No one had a clue.

When summer arrived, things started to take a dramatic turn-around with Judy. She found a part-time job which she really enjoyed. She even started talking to the other family members around the dinner table.

However, her manner of dress remained unchanged. Her daily uniform consisted of dirty cut-offs and T-shirt. And she still left the house each morning with wet, stringy hair. Caroline resisted the constant temptation to say something about her appearance, telling herself to be thankful instead for the positive changes in other areas of Judy's life.

As school approached, Caroline cautiously offered her services in helping Judy pick out her school clothes for the fall. When Judy didn't take her up on the offer, she lightly suggested that Judy might want to use the credit card some time to buy her clothes and that the card would be on her dresser when she needed it. With great restraint, Caroline said nothing further, not even daring to check to see if the card had been used.

The day before school started, nothing was said about clothes by either Caroline or Judy. Other years, what to wear the first day of school was the great point of discussion among Judy and her friends and between Judy and Caroline. The next morning confirmed Caroline's worst fears as Judy appeared ready for school in the same dirty cut-offs and T-shirt she'd slept in, with her hair stringy and wet.

When Judy announced she was ready for school, Caroline swallowed hard and said nothing. They got into the car and picked up several of Judy's friends on the way to school. Each stop produced a young lady dressed beautifully in her new fall clothes.

After dropping the girls off at school, Caroline sat in her car and watched as the other kids arrived. No one was dressed like Judy! She sat there and wondered aloud, "Why would she want to look like that? She sticks out like a sore thumb."

Caroline and her husband coped so well. Somehow they knew when to keep quiet. But they were to face another whole year in which they were to learn again that all they could do was to provide a loving atmosphere in which Judy could rebel. They had to remind themselves countless times that there really was a person behind the behavior.

❋   ❋   ❋

How does one understand Judy's behavior, especially when she wasn't even conforming to the standards of her peers? We have to accept the fact that there was purpose in her behavior. All behavior is purposive, and Judy was actively interacting with her environment. She was acting on the basis of her own subjective interpretation of reality.

We each have a "private logic" which determines how we decide to behave in any given situation. The resulting behavior, which seems best to us, may appear to be completely illogical to others, especially when it is the behavior of a child being observed by his parents. We may never understand the private logic behind Judy's behavior those two years, but accepting the fact that she had rational reasons for her behavior, which made sense to her at the time, helped her parents see beyond her behavior and continue to accept her as a person.

This does not mean we ignore behavior, or allow destructive behavior to go unchallenged. Ignoring behavior would make the parent a passive observer. And no matter how much we might relish the thought of such a position, we cannot escape our responsibility as parents and our active involvement in our children's behavior—be it good or bad.

Dismissing behavior *does* mean that we never use our children's behavior as a basis for evaluating their worth as a person. Behavior is temporary, and is based on each individual's perception of reality. And no two people ever perceive reality as being the same. If every time we faced a crisis with one of our children we could remember that his perception of the situation is different from ours, we might be able to see beyond the behavior in question, and step back for a more objective look at what's going on.

The problem of hair is a good example. Long hair on young men has probably caused more family quarrels during the past decade than any other single subject. Hair is about the only thing we have left, except for clothing, with which to say, "Hey, look at me!" Hair sends a message—especially to parents.

Brad was one of those kids who let his hair grow and grow and grow, much to the distress of his father. It always seems to offend Dad more than anyone else. As Brad's hair grew past his shoulders, Joe, his father, started his campaign in earnest. Every night at dinner, somehow the subject of conversation got around to Brad's hair. Subtle suggestions like, "Why don't you make an appointment and have your hair *styled?*" soon gave way to direct threats like, "If you don't get your hair cut you can't use the car this weekend!" Joe offered all kinds of bribes, and made all kinds of threats, all ineffective. Brad's hair kept growing.

Joe looked upon Brad's hair as a symbol of rebellion. After all, long hair on men was a symbol of rebellion during the Viet Nam War. We forget that up until World War I, long hair on men was stylish. We also forget that since the days of the Viet Nam War, middle-class America has picked up this protest symbol and converted it into a stylish fad. But Brad had his own way of thinking, based on his own "private logic" and neither Joe nor anyone else could be sure if the length of Brad's hair was a symbol of protest or an expression of personal taste. Joe's task is not to try to figure out Brad's private logic, but to realize there is a person behind that long hair—hang on to HIM.

❦　　❦　　❦

It's never easy to dismiss behavior this way, for behavior is always at the core of broken relationships. Oh, how we wish we could've been able to see beyond behavior with Jeff, particularly when his behavior caused so much pain. At times we did see the person behind the behavior, and in those very special moments we were able to experience the power of this principle.

❋   ❋   ❋

Jeff had been away from home for almost two weeks. We had restored communication with him, but made no efforts to force him to return home. Jan was usually away from home working on Monday mornings, but this particular Monday morning her staff meeting was unexpectedly cancelled. When she returned home from the office early, she walked in on a very surprised son and his friend, gathering armloads of items from his room. Apparently they didn't hear the car pull in, for Jan was upstairs facing them in the hall before they had a chance to even hide. Jan thought of all kinds of good things to say later, but at the moment she could only say, "Put the stereo back. You're not taking it anywhere. Just what do you think you're doing?"

Jeff glared back at her and sharply said, "Are you finished? Can we go now?" With that he and his friend made their way downstairs, through the kitchen and out the back door. Jan stood there for a moment, stunned, and then looked around to see what else they might have taken. In the kitchen she found the remains of what looked like a number of sandwiches they had hurriedly made and eaten. Sitting down, she thought to herself, "Why didn't I accept him lovingly and ask how he was doing or if he was hungry?" He looked like he had lost a lot of weight those two weeks. Soon the thought that he was starving and the realization of how bad he must be hurting really got to Jan.

Just then, she looked up and saw Jeff and his friend sneaking around the back of the house to retrieve something hidden by the garbage cans. As she watched from a window, it broke her heart to see that what they had "stolen" was four half-gallons of milk. Why did our own son think he had to steal milk from his own family? What kind of private logic was he using to make such a decision? Didn't he know that the milk was his and that we loved him and wanted him home?

The desperateness of Jeff's behavior forced us to face the fact that there must have been things he perceived in his relationship to us that caused him to make the choice to behave like he did. That evening we talked at length about what took place, and Jan worried about how she could have handled it differently. But then we started to focus on Jeff's feelings and needs, and for the first time in several years we were able to see the person behind the behavior. His way of thinking and interpreting life—his private logic—was very different from ours. Looking back, that event was a turning point in our attitude towards Jeff. And we thought we knew what unconditional love was all about. We sure had a lot more to learn!

Sometimes, the only way to hang on to the person behind the behavior is to force that person to face the consequences of his behavior. After all, we are an influence and a guide—we still have a responsibility as parents.

Larry's behavior became more mysterious every week. His mother Ann had conscientiously struggled to raise her children alone. Her husband had left when they were young. Up until a year ago, she felt she was on the right track in spite of the necessity for her to spend long hours away from home working.

Larry had started to run around with some kids she didn't feel comfortable about. They neither worked nor went to school. Larry attended classes at the local junior college, but had no friends there. Soon he was cutting classes to spend time with his new friends, and his grades were beginning to suffer.

Ann was a mother who really tried to understand the feelings of her kids. She was very open and honest with them about her own struggles and, as a result, enjoyed open communication with each of her children. But Larry was shutting her out of his life, and it seemed to be more than just the natural "growing apart" that comes with the struggle for independence.

One day as she was cleaning his room, she discovered that he was gathering quite a collection of car radios and stereos. For several weeks she wondered where they came from but put off asking, for fear she might get an answer she couldn't handle.

Several weeks later, she checked his collection again, and found there had been a turnover in merchandise. Her worst fears seemed confirmed, and finally she confronted Larry. He defiantly told her, "I stole them. And it's none of your business."

How do you dismiss that behavior? Ann struggled with what her response should be. Since Larry was over eighteen, there was a good chance he would have to go to jail if he was caught. She wondered, "How can a parent turn her kid into the police and still live with herself? Maybe he'll see how wrong it is and return the stuff." But as she prayed and thought about her choices, she knew what she had to do. In order to salvage the person, Larry was going to have to face the consequences of his behavior. She called the police.

Ann stood there weeping as the police led Larry away, handcuffed. She didn't know whether he'd ever speak to her again or even if she would see him again, for she could feel his hatred as he glared at her.

Larry did go to jail for sixty days, and after he got out, he didn't come home. But Ann kept praying, confident she had done the right thing.

Two years later, Larry returned home with a smile on his face, asking for his mother's forgiveness. He told her how after he got out of jail, he became involved with a Christian group that confronted him with his need to face responsibility for his own behavior. Within the fellowship of that group, he experienced forgiveness as he opened his life to a relationship with Jesus Christ.

Ann's actions are a good example of how a parent can resist the temptation to ignore behavior while at the same time dismissing that behavior. It's clear that Ann did not ignore Larry's behavior. But we can say that she did dismiss his behavior because she did not allow that misbehavior to become the basis for her relationship with him, or use it as a barrier that blocked her love for him. Her unconditional love for Larry was the base from which she worked as she helped him face the consequences of his misbehavior.

Just think what our relationship to God would be like if his love for us depended on our behavior. One day he might love us and the next he might not—depending on what we did. Obviously, God does not ignore our behavior. But he does not dole out or hold back his love for us according to our behavior. His example of unconditional love serves as the model for us as we explore what it means in our family relationships.

🌿　　🌿　　🌿

A young father had two daughters.*

As the years went by, he watched them grow up through "Captain Kangaroo" and skate boards, the new math, gold eye shadow and a bewildering series of diets. They teased each other, fought some, and increasingly took for granted their life together at 205 Woodfield Place.

---

*"A Tale of Two Sisters," by Hope Warwick, reprinted by permission from *Campus Life* magazine, ©1972, Youth for Christ International, Wheaton, Illinois.

One day when the youngest was sixteen, she decided she could do without homework and curfews and the endless mother-daughter hassles over what to wear and who to go with.

So she stuffed an extra pair of Levis into her sleeping bag, cashed in two government bonds she'd been given to save toward college, and hiked about three miles down an abandoned railroad track to the outskirts of town. At dusk, she cut across a vacant lot to the freeway and hitched the first of five rides between her Pittsburgh suburb and New York.

Police couldn't trace her. And every runaway organization her parents managed to contact could give no information.

In the city, she blew all she had on a one-month stint in a dingy hotel and on other unfun things like food, an extra blanket, a red nylon parka, and deodorant.

There was no homework.

When she ran out of money, a group of kids she'd gotten in with offered her a damp corner of their basement room.

She discovered that pot made her sick (dizzy, vomiting sick), and though it embarrassed her to no end, she never tried other drugs after that. She discovered, too, that these new transient friends used her as thoroughly and callously as the kids and teachers back home had seemed to.

Her sleeping bag got moldy.

For two weeks she wandered around downtown Manhattan, checked out "Help Wanted, Female" ads, but no luck. She bought a different paper then and sat down at one of the back booths of a greasy pizza joint to read more ads. Her feet hurt . . . both heels were blistered. She had a head-ache.

She thought about the dark, eight-block walk to her corner room and decided she was going home. So she called her dad, and he wired money for plane fare, even for a taxi to the airport, though she told him she could take a bus.

Early the next morning on board Alle-gheny's flight 841, she let down her seat as far as it would go and slept deeply.

Her dad had somehow gotten through the Passengers Only gate and he met her on the runway. Not once did he accuse her of hurt-ing him, and she knew he never would.

Out in the parking lot, he led her to a '68 VW.

"You've come down in status," she said. "Did you sell your Buick?"

"No. This one's yours." He gave her the keys and hugged her hard. He was trembling, and she could recall having seen him so deeply moved only once before; when her mom came out of surgery and they said it wasn't cancer. "It could probably stand a paint job, but we thought you needed something to get around in."

Twenty minutes later, she pushed open the back door and walked into the warm, coppery kitchen. Bacon was frying, and the coffee had just started to perk, slowly, with uneven rhythm.

Her sister slipped quietly into the family room, turned on the TV, and sat waiting for the test pattern to fade into an early morning talk show. She felt cheated, pushed aside. The happy reunion chatter in the kitchen ground into her stomach. What did all her attempts at being an ideal daughter mean anyway?

A few minutes later, when her dad came in to call her to breakfast, the nagging hurt inside her spilled out. "Okay, I don't claim to be perfect, but at least I've stayed home and done darn near every cruddy thing you've ever asked, and you never even say, 'Thank you.' I slaved in a restaurant to buy *my* car. Now *she* comes dragging back here, a washed-out little street-sleeper who's blown her college savings and put you through hell, and you—you're *glad!*"

He stared at her for a long time, as though willing her to understand. "Our love for you is stronger than ever. But it's a time for joy! Your sister's back. If we couldn't forgive each other, we'd have no home.

Aspects of this story sound familiar? See Luke 15:11-32.)

7

Changing
the Rules
of the Game

"When you're down in a deep rut, you see only the sides. You forget there's a big world up above. Somehow you've got to get into the sunshine above the rut. The aerial view gives you a better idea about how to get out."

Tim Stafford
The Trouble With Parents

There are so many messed up families around today that we tend to forget that God had something better in mind. Of course, there are no perfect families just as there are no simple formulas. But there are some ideals which I can aim for that get me into the sunshine. From that perspective I have a better view of my rut and I might see some steps that will lead me out.

One of the deepest ruts a parent can get caught in is the use of punishment as an attempt to influence behavior. This is not a treatise against the use of punishment, for there are times when it is appropriate. But as the child becomes an adolescent, the old forms of punishment are no longer effective. After all, what good does it do to spank your son when he's 6'4" and weighs 175 pounds? That's when many parents start to resort to the use of "grounding" or placing some other similar restriction on the young person's activities. This form of punishment only serves to drive a kid to discover all kinds of creative ways to become immune to its effects.

Sharon was grounded for two weeks and each evening immediately following dinner she closed herself in her room to listen to her stereo. Her parents thought she was taking her punishment pretty well. But soon after turning on the stereo, she would climb out of her bedroom window and visit with friends—somehow managing to return before her parents checked in on her. She almost carried it off. Her parents didn't discover her nightly escapades until the second week.

For the kid not brazen enough to sneak out the window, the stereo can make solitary confinement quite tolerable. If the stereo is placed off limits, magazines or a retreat to his private fantasy world helps the time pass quickly. And how does a parent cope with that? Longer restrictions? We tried that—to no avail. We also discovered that grounding often grounds the parents as well, which only tempts us to cut the restriction short.

Taking away a kid's means of transportation can sometimes be effective until he works out an exchange system with his friends to help each other out in times of crisis.

If punishment doesn't do the job, some parents resort to the use of guilt as a means of controlling their child's behavior. As we were discussing our ideas for this chapter, our youngest son, who is quick to express his insights, reminded Jan of the Easter morning when she actually admitted that she had used every trick in the book—including laying on a guilt trip—in her effort to get our oldest son to go to church with us. We both sat there, silently thinking of the many times we had tried to use guilt as a means of influencing our boys behavior, and had very little success. We also thought of the mother who, at one point of exasperation, angrily said to her daughter, "Your misbehavior was the main reason your dad and I got divorced." What a burden to place on a child! Trying to make our children feel guilty is only an attempt to pretend we can be their conscience—an impossibility, no matter how much we wish it could be true.

Some parents resort to withholding money, affection, attention, and approval in their attempts to change behavior. I'm sure our boys could remind us of times we tried each of these techniques. Looking back, we're struck most with the futility of those efforts. Our experience at punishing our teenagers has only served to add to our frustration and seldom has had any lasting effect on their behavior.

If parents and children alike are to survive, the outer pressures of punishment must be replaced by something that will motivate the child from within. Most adult behavior is not motivated by a fear of punishment. It is motivated by the knowledge that every act has a consequence. But for the young child growing up, it is only the process of maturing that gradually teaches him to anticipate or predict these consequences. Wouldn't it be great if there was some way we could hurry-up the maturing process. We could probably erase from our vocabulary that much-used phrase, "You should have known better!" Wow! Would that ever make the task of parenting easier!

❀   ❀   ❀

Jan remembers the many times she sat in the park watching our boys, when they were small, wander around the play area. Like most every other child there, they were intrigued with the bigger kids on the swings.

Again and again, Jan would run over, pull one of them away, and say, "Don't stand so close. You'll get hit by the swing!" All she needed to do was turn her back for one minute and the howls of pain told her that the inevitable had happened.

A few moments of comforting turned off the flood of tears, and soon he was back watching the swings. Only this time, he kept a safe distance, and Jan didn't have to say another word. He was gradually learning by the process of trial and error that his actions often have natural consequences that could be avoided.

❀   ❀   ❀

Piaget, a French psychologist who has spent his lifetime studying the development of children, has shown in his studies that children do not have the ability to anticipate the results of their behavior. Their minds simply do not have the reasoning ability necessary to make such judgments.

In one of his experiments with early elementary grade children, Piaget had two clear plastic jars sitting on a shelf, filled with the same amount of liquid. Attached to each of these jars was a tube leading down to two other jars on a lower shelf. One tube led to a short, wide jar; the other tube led to a tall, narrow jar.

The child watched as the same amount of liquid was released from each of the top jars. Because these were identical jars, the amount of liquid in one jar remained level with the other. But because of the shape of the jars below, the levels of liquid were different.

The child was asked to point to the jar on the lower shelf that had the most liquid in it. He invariably pointed to the tall, narrow jar. His answer was based on his perception that the level of the liquid in the tall, thin jar was higher than the level of the liquid in the short, wide jar. He reached this conclusion even though he could look at the jars above and see that equal amounts of liquid had been released. He had that information, but his perception of reality led him to the wrong answer.

This inability of the child to perceive the conservation of volume is only one example of his limited reasoning ability. The child makes choices through a system of trial and error, based on his unreliable perception of reality. As he matures and experiences the natural consequences of his actions, he will gradually learn to anticipate those consequences.

❀   ❀   ❀

One of the ideals that brought us up into the sunshine was a form of discipline set forth by Rudolf Dreikurs* which he calls "logical consequences." Logical conse-

_____

* Rudolf Dreikurs and Loren Grey, *A New Approach to Discipline: Logical Consequences*, New York, Hawthorn Books, 1968.

quences are defined as situations where the consequences of misbehavior are arranged by the parent or another adult. Natural consequences, like the example of our son being hit in the back by a swing, *naturally* follow ill-advised acts. If misbehavior does not produce an immediate *natural* consequence that is directly related to that behavior, then a parent can arrange a *logical consequence* that will have the same effect. *Without logical* consequences, the corrective effect on misbehavior may be lost.

Helping our child face the consequences of his actions does not mean we expose him to danger, just so that he can learn what his behavior brings. But there is a delicate balance between protecting a child from danger and sheltering a child from the results of his behavior. In retrospect, we can see that it was very easy for us to believe we were protecting our children from potential harm, either physical or emotional, when in reality we were bailing them out of a jam that they *should* have worked themselves out of. And we were sheltering them from the consequences of their own behavior. As a result, their process of maturing was hindered.

Ouch—here comes the guilt again. I could have done it better. Of course I could have!

As the clouds of guilt start to hide the recently discovered sunshine, I quickly remind myself that the past is past. I can only affect the present. Regardless of the age of my children, I can still change the way the game is played, even if they're away from home or married. *Each new day offers the possibility of a fresh new beginning.*

❊   ❊   ❊

We were experimenting with some of these ideas in our family and had some interesting results. We were seeing that most of the misbehavior in our family was either an attempt to attract attention or the desire to gain power. As we stepped back and allowed our boys to face for themselves the results of their behavior, we found that the struggle for power was greatly reduced.

Jan walked out of the house one day and found Jeff busily taking off the new tires and rims from the front of his truck. They had been a birthday present and had replaced a set of bald tires and rusty old wheels. Jan's natural response was to ask, "Why are you doing that?" He responded with a funny little smile and said, "I don't have the money to get the front-end fixed and I don't want to ruin these tires. I'm putting the old ones back on until I can get the front-end fixed."

Jan couldn't believe her ears. She rushed into the family room and exclaimed, "It works! It works!" We had been bugging Jeff for over two weeks to take the truck into the garage and get the front-end fixed. And the demand always included the words, "Do it today!" Each evening, Jeff would non-chalantly inform us, "I didn't have time today. I'll take care of it tomorrow."

After about a week of such verbal exchanges, we started to realize that we had been sucked into a power struggle with Jeff. Who was going to win? Obviously he had the upper hand, for he was the one delaying taking any action to fix the front-end of the truck. And each day he delayed, he was scoring a victory in the battle of wills.

This encounter took place while we were discussing ways to help our boys face the responsibility for their behavior. We were tired of their attitude that seemed to say that if something was broken, ruined or lost, it didn't matter, for it could be replaced. Mom or Dad will take care of it. And we were also facing the harsh truth that *we* were the ones that had allowed that atti-tude to develop.

We decided to withdraw from the conflict by firmly announcing to Jeff, "The tires are yours to do with what you want." For the next three days, nothing more was said on the subject. We stopped bugging him about the truck. Four days later Jan saw him changing the tires.

※　　※　　※

That was just a minor episode, but it gave us the courage to try to withdraw from verbal conflict in other areas. A parent cannot be firm when he keeps on talking. And I have a tendency to do just that. I keep talking, thinking I can convince my sons to see things my way. Or I try to talk them out of their anger or talk them through some disappointment. I have painfully discovered that talking only increases the conflict. Just when I think I have talked one of them out of something—or into doing something—and I sit back and relax, I find him back in the room trying to reopen negotiations. And there I am, talking again.

The more any parent talks, the more he sets himself up as an authority. Whenever an adolescent encounters an authority figure, there is a power struggle. And a struggle for power diverts attention away from the realities of the situation.

As the struggle for power intensifies, respect for the other person is diminished. Dreikurs points out that the best formula for the proper attitude in avoiding a power struggle with children is to treat them with kindness and firmness. He says, "*Kindness* expresses respect *for* the child and firmness evokes respect *from* the child." Many parents are kind and firm, but seldom at the same time. The trick is to get them working together.

Not only does the use of logical consequences defuse the struggle for power between parent and adolescent, it also helps the child relate the consequences directly to his misbehavior. Punishment is usually related to the angry or hurt emotions of the parent. For a child, these intense emotions within his parents only serve to divert his attention away from his misbehavior. The use of logical consequences confronts the child directly with the result of his misbehavior.

※　　※　　※

The phone rang in our motel room. We were startled, for the only people who knew where we were, were back home. The voice on the phone identified himself as Jeff's probation officer. He informed us that Jeff had been picked up by the police the night before and was being held in Juvenile Hall.

We were several thousand miles from home on a vacation which we had planned for some time. Jeff was supposed to have been with us—in fact, that was one of the main reasons in planning the vacation. He had expressed a real desire to go with us, and we looked forward to spending the time together as a family.

But a week before we were to leave, Jeff left home again—for no reason that we could understand—and we had no idea where he was or who he was with. We had thought seriously about canceling our plans, and at one point we did. But then we thought, "No, that's exactly what Jeff expects us to do, for he was aware we were willing to do almost anything that would keep the family together."

We reconfirmed our reservations and left without knowing where Jeff was. We kept thinking each day we would get a call from the gal staying at our house telling us Jeff had come home. Jan even entertained thoughts of wiring him a ticket if he came home, so that he could join us. That would have been the easy thing to do but hardly a good example of using logical consequences.

But we never thought about receiving this type of call. The probation officer told us they would have to hold Jeff until we, or some other adult relative could come and pick him up. We took down the information and thanked him for letting us know.

Now what should we do? Our first

thought was to get on a plane and head for home immediately, so we could rescue him from that horrible place. That's what we usually did. But this time we resisted that urge and sat down and discussed how we could use logical consequences in this situation. We made the decision to stay, even though we wavered a bit during the next three days and made several phone calls to ask some friends to stop and check on him.

As we talked with him later, we knew we had made the right decision. We realized that in this situation, he clearly saw that the consequences he faced were directly related to his misbehavior. We were impressed with the fact that nothing more needed to be said and *we didn't feel guilty*. The consequences spoke for themselves.

※　　※　　※

Another advantage of using logical consequences is that it involves no element of moral judgment on the part of the parent. There is a distinction made between the action and the person behind the action. Traditionally, punishment has also conveyed the message, "You have misbehaved, therefore you are a bad person." Self-esteem is torn down in the process.

Facing the consequences of any behavior

helps us build feelings of confidence and self-respect. It allows a person the freedom to decide for himself whether or not he wants to repeat a certain action. It also frees the parent to develop the attitude that the child is a person of equal worth, and it encourages the growth of positive self-esteem. This is especially important in the discussion of sticky moral issues. The absence of a judgmental attitude that allows other people the freedom to be wrong encourages the growth of reciprocity and fairness—both essential to moral development and maturity.

But isn't this just another success formula for parenting? Maybe it appears that way, but we have found it to be more than that. It presents a whole different basis for relationships and allows for the complex differences in the individuals involved. For each person becomes the one responsible for the consequences of *his own* behavior— including parents.

Because it forces individual responsibility for behavior, it isn't an easy solution. We've found it's hard for us to change; we've been down in the rut too long. It's hard to leave a kid's room a mess and let him live with it, or to wash his socks inside out—like he left them—and put them away that way. It's even harder to know your child is sitting in what we found out was the roughest juvenile hall in the county—and not rush to his rescue.

But the more we practice logical consequences as a way of handling the misbehavior of our kids, the more we find ourselves getting off the hook and enjoying guilt-free relationships.

8

Getting
Off the Hook—
Guilt-Free
Relationships

*"Stop your anger! Turn off your wrath.
Don't fret and worry—it only leads to
harm . . . Rest in the Lord!"*

From Psalm 37
The Living Bible

When it finally comes down to the day-by-day realities of my life as a parent, it takes more than the application of logical consequences to create guilt-free relationships. There are times when the anger and the fret and the worry and the hurt build to the point where you say, "Lord, I can't take any more!"

Julie really hadn't created many problems for her parents. She had gone through the typical teenage moodiness, but she was open and responsive to both her parents and seemed to have things pretty much under control. But the last six weeks her moods began to fluctuate dramatically, and the infrequent conflicts with her parents became a daily occurence.

Then suddenly, she dropped the bomb. After a violent confrontation with her mother, she started to sob. And between her sobs, she blurted out the words, "I'm pregnant!"

Nothing in the world could have prepared Julie's parents for the hurt and anger that overwhelmed them both. How does a parent apply logical consequences in that kind of situation? Do they encourage her to have the baby? Do they encourage her to keep the baby and marry the father—at age sixteen? Or do they insist she get an abortion?

When faced with decisions that carry such long-term consequences and involve such moral issues, a parent is called upon to exercise wisdom which none of us possess. In such an irreversible situation, the need to hang on to the person behind the behavior is critical, and only unconditional love can fill that need. Wow! If we'd have known in advance that we would be faced with demands like these, how many of us would have had kids?

There will always be times when a parent can't make the pain go away, or make wrong things right. But Psalm 37 shows us how we can still survive, and how we can keep on living:

> "Fret not yourself because of the wicked,
> be not envious of wrongdoers!

For they will soon fade like the grass,
  and wither like the green herb.
Trust in the Lord, and do good;
  so you will dwell in the land,
  and enjoy security.
Take delight in the Lord,
  and he will give you the desires
  of your heart.
Commit your way to the Lord;
  trust in him and he will act.
He will bring forth your vindication
  as the light, and your right as
  the noonday.
Be still before the Lord, and wait
  patiently for him;
Fret not yourself . . . .

Psalm 37:1-7, RSV

The psalmist David builds a progression of thought in these verses that holds the key to maintaining guilt-free relationships. There are four familiar words that sum up what he is saying: Commit, trust, delight and rest. Parenting is an impossible task without the understanding and application of these principles.

As young Christian parents dedicating our boys to the Lord, we had no idea what that would mean as they grew up. As the years have unfolded, we've found that it takes a daily, and sometimes a moment-by-moment act of commitment, trusting that

God is at work in their lives—and that includes committing to God every kind of behavior possible. Oh how difficult that is in the middle of the night when you don't know where your son is or what he's doing! At those times, if I can discipline myself to verbalize the commitment—even when the feelings are absent—release comes.

Taking delight in the Lord goes one step beyond trusting and committing to the point of being able to say, "Lord, not only do I entrust him to you, but I can also rejoice in the fact that You are involved in each situation and I will praise You for it." Again, when I verbalize my praise, it forces me to shift the focus of my attention and energy away from the problem. Even in the middle of the worst circumstances, I can still praise God and rejoice.

The act of resting is vividly described by the psalmist as being *still* before the Lord and *waiting patiently* for him to do his thing. As I rest in the Lord, my anger can subside and my worries cease, for He is the one responsible for the end results.

But rest is difficult for me, for I am an impatient person, frequently trying to force my timetable on God's plans. Yet so often something will happen that reminds me I cannot manipulate God, and as I wait patiently for him to act, I enjoy a renewed objectivity regarding the circumstances.

When I am in a position of rest and enjoy the objectivity that comes with it, I have a whole different perspective about myself and my relationships. For one thing, I can see that all the responses and emotions that I have tried to blame on circumstances and other people's behavior are the result of my choices. I chose to respond that way! I have only myself to blame if I feel angry, hurt or disappointed. I can only be upset if I allow myself to be. Even in the worst circumstances, *I can choose to focus on the hope!*

> I CAN CHOOSE TO
> FOCUS ON THE HURT,
> OR I CAN CHOOSE TO
> FOCUS ON THE HOPE.

Even Julie's parents, in the example at the beginning of the chapter, have a number of choices about how to respond. They can become angry and send Julie away to a special home for unwed mothers. They can choose to respond with feelings of disappointment and hurt over the shattered dreams and hopes they had for their daughter, saying to themselves, "How could she do this to us!" But there is also the choice of responding in a way that focuses

on Julie's needs and God's involvement—
even in this! With this choice comes the
possibility of turning it into a positive growing experience for both Julie and themselves.

This sheds a whole new light on my relationship with my kids. It takes the tension
away from the relationship because I can
stop being an emotional yo-yo. I have the
right to choose how I am going to respond to
whatever my child does, and nothing or no
one can take that right away from me!

If I have that right, I must also recognize
that my children have the same right. They
make choices about their own behavior.
They are unique, thinking, human beings,
who, based on their perceptions of their
world, exercise their own will and make
decisions about how to respond. They are
responsible for their behavior; they are also
responsible for facing the consequences of
that behavior—*I'M OFF THE HOOK!*

As I accept the responsibility for my
actions and emotional responses, and allow
my children to do the same, I escape the
trap of guilt and discover that I can experience the freedom to love in spite of the
behavior. And isn't that where the joy of
parenting lies—in loving? That's exciting!
Now all that's left is to live it.

. . . it's 3:00 a.m. Jeff still isn't home.

Thank you, Lord, for what you are doing in his life—even when I don't understand it all. He's in your hands. Do it your way and in your time . . . .

Join the movement! Display your own bumper sticker, or put one on your kid's car. Parents also need to be hugged. So order yours today.

HAVE YOU HUGGED YOUR PARENTS TODAY?

THE TOTAL(ED) PARENT — PUBLISHED BY HARVEST HOUSE, IRVINE, CA 92714

------------------------------ cut ------------------------------

Harvest House Publishers
2861 McGaw Avenue
Irvine, California 92714

Please send me (in quantities of 2 or more) _____ of the HAVE YOU HUGGED YOUR PARENTS TODAY? bumper stickers at $1.00 each. Enclosed is my check or money order for $_____.

NAME _____
         (please print)
ADDRESS _____

CITY_____ STATE_____ ZIP____

OTHER GOOD HARVEST HOUSE READING

☐ **TURNING YOUR STRESS INTO STRENGTH.** On his internationally acclaimed television program, the HOUR OF POWER, Dr. Robert H. Schuller has interviewed men and women from every walk of life. Through their experiences, Dr. Schuller shares positive and powerful principles which you can use to turn your stress into strength. 113X—$2.95 (paper)

☐ **BUILDING POSITIVE PARENT-TEEN RELATIONSHIPS,** Norman Wright and Rex Johnson. A complete teaching guide. This unique learning experience for parents and youth contains over twenty hours of Bible-based teaching materials. Designed to be taught by anyone in fifteen sessions. The contents of the course have been adapted from seminars held across the country. Complete with twelve color overhead transparencies and twelve reproduction masters. To be used with the student books: COMMUNICATION—KEY TO YOUR PARENTS and COMMUNICATION—KEY TO YOUR TEENS. 1482—$9.95 (8½ x 11 paper)

☐ **COMMUNICATION—KEY TO YOUR PARENTS,** Teen Guide, Rex Johnson. Teenagers can do something constructive to rebuild the patterns of communication with their family. This book considers questions like what to do with problem parents and how to find a safe way to relate to them. May be read independent of the teacher's manual or as a text for the course: BUILDING POSITIVE PARENT-TEEN RELATIONSHIP. 1571—$2.95 (paper)

☐ **COMMUNICATION—KEY TO YOUR TEENS,** Parent Guide, Norman Wright and Rex Johnson. Practical suggestions and guidelines for improving and maintaining communication with your teenagers. This book considers questions like what makes a good parent and how to develop trust in your teenager. May be read independent of the teacher's manual or as a text for the course: BUILDING POSITIVE PARENT-TEEN RELATIONSHIPS 158X—$2.95 (paper)

☐ **HELP ME LORD—I HURT!,** Virginia Thompson. A collection of prayers set to poetry and highlighted by beautiful and sensitive drawings. Here are prayers for the dark hours of loneliness in the middle of the night; prayers for the uncertain moments as children move into adulthood; and prayers for the practical moments of hurt in anyone's life. 1458—$1.95 (mass paper)

☐ **PARENTS: GIVE YOUR KID A CHANCE,** Ken Poure and Dave Stoop. Here are positive steps you can take to help your children find, develop and fulfill their God-given potential. Prepare your kids for their future. Regardless of their ages you can now make a vital difference in their lives. This book offers hope for your family today. 0680—$2.95 (paper)

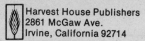
Harvest House Publishers
2861 McGaw Ave.
Irvine, California 92714